J.S. BACH

SHEEP MAY SAFELY GRAZE

Schafe können sicher weiden

Transcribed for piano solo
by Mary Howe

OXFORD
UNIVERSITY PRESS

SCHAFE KÖNNEN SICHER WEIDEN

(SHEEP MAY SAFELY GRAZE)

NOTE

This arrangement has been made from a Soprano Recitative and Aria from the Birthday Cantata by Bach for Herzog Christian zu Sachsen-Weissenfels, called 'Was mir behagt ist nur die muntre Jagd' (My only delight is the merry chase).

Transcribed for Piano by
MARY HOWE

J. S. BACH

Andante Pastorale
(Ruhig)

con Ped.

simile.

ben cantando

dim.

p esp. dolce
marcato il canto

cresc.

dim.

3

OXFORD UNIVERSITY PRESS

OXFORD
UNIVERSITY PRESS

www.oup.com

ISBN 978-0-19-387081-9

9 780193 870819